Retirement

COLORING BOOK

This book belongs to:

____

JOB DESCRIPTION:
CAN'T
BE BOTHERED

MY JOB?!
you mean relaxing?!

JUST LEAF me ALONE

RETIREMENT
TASTES
great

DRAMA
LLAMA?
MORE LIKE RETIRED
LLAMA!

Exercise?
You mean take another nap?

TIME
FLIES
when you're retired

Tired?
MORE LIKE
RETIRED!

RETIRED OR NOT
I'M STILL NUTS

NO LONGER
as busy
AS A BEE!

I'm not
FISH BAIT
ANYMORE

NO MORE
BLOODSUCKING
FOR ME

NO
I'M OUT OF THE
RAT RACE
NOW
I've retired

I'M MUCH LESS
CRABBY
SINCE
RETIREMENT

I've done a lot of HANGING OUT
SINCE I'VE RETIRED

OH DEER
WHAT WILL I DO
WITH ALL OF THIS TIME?

I'M JUST
WILD
FOR RETIREMENT

RETIREMENT
IS a WHALE
OF
a GOOD TIME!

I COULDN'T BEAR ANOTHER DAY OF WORK

RETIREMENT
has me
JUMPING
FOR
JOY

RETIREMENT
THE LONGEST COFFEE
BREAK

FOX TROTTING
to the bank

I REMEMBER HOW
TRASHY
COMMUTING WAS

Retirement
IT'S GRRREAT

Made in the USA
Las Vegas, NV
30 April 2022

48191856R10031